Book 2

Literature & Comprehension

Writing Skills

Language Arts

Assessments

K12

A Stride Company

Book Staff and Contributors

Kristen Kinney-Haines   *Director, Primary Literacy*
Marianne Murphy   *Senior Content Specialist*
Anna Day   *Director, Instructional Design for Language Arts and History/Social Studies*
Frances Suazo   *Senior Instructional Designer*
Cheryl Howard   *Instructional Designer*
Karen Ingebretsen   *Text Editor*
Suzanne Montazer   *Creative Director, Print and ePublishing*
Jayoung Cho   *Senior Print Visual Designer*
Stephanie Shaw Williams   *Cover Designer*
Karen Draper   *Lead Assessment Specialist*
Joshua Briggs, Tisha Ruibal   *Writers*
Amy Eward   *Senior Manager, Writers*
Susan Raley   *Senior Manager, Editors*
Deanna Lacek   *Project Manager*
David Johnson   *Director, Program Management Grades K–8*

Maria Szalay   *Executive Vice President, Product Development*
John Holdren   *Senior Vice President, Content and Curriculum*
David Pelizzari   *Vice President, K¹² Content*
Kim Barcas   *Vice President, Creative*
Laura Seuschek   *Vice President, Assessment and Research*
Christopher Frescholtz   *Senior Director, Program Management*
Lisa Dimaio Iekel   *Director, Print Production and Manufacturing*
Ray Traugott   *Production Manager*

Illustrations Credits

All illustrations © Stride, Inc. unless otherwise noted

978-1-60153-215-2
Printed by Action Printing, Fond du Lac, WI, USA, May 2021.

Contents

Literature & Comprehension

Writing Skills

Literature & Comprehension

Mid-Semester Checkpoint Learning Coach Instructions Shared Reading Comprehension and Analysis

Explain that students are going to show what they have learned so far this semester.

- Give students pages LC 73–LC 106 of the Mid-Semester Checkpoint.
- Read the directions on the students' pages together. Use the Learning Coach instructions on pages LC 67–LC 72 to administer the Checkpoint.
- Use the Checkpoint pages to record student behaviors and responses.
- When you have finished, use the Answer Key to score the Checkpoint and then enter the results online.
- Review each exercise with students. Work with students to correct any exercise that they missed.

Part 1. Fiction: "A Trip to the Magic Sea" Activate Prior Knowledge

Ask students the following questions to activate prior knowledge. Note their responses on the Checkpoint pages.

1. Have you ever been bored?

2. What did you do for fun when you were bored?

Before reading "A Trip to the Magic Sea," go over Words to Know with students. Read aloud each word or phrase and have students repeat it. Ask students if they know what each word or phrase means.

- If students know a word's or phrase's meaning, have them define it and use it in a sentence.
- If students don't know a word's or phrase's meaning, read them the definition and discuss the word or phrase with them.

bored – weary or restless; dull
paper airplane – a piece of paper folded to look like a toy airplane

Part 2. Fiction: "A Trip to the Magic Sea" Book Walk

Gather the Checkpoint pages with "A Trip to the Magic Sea." Note that there are two versions of the story: One is the full story for the students, and one is a copy for you to follow and mark as the students read aloud. Have students sit next to you so that they can see the story while you do a Book Walk. Read aloud the title and author of the text. Show students the illustration. Ask students the following questions and note their responses on the Checkpoint pages.

3. What do you think the story will be about?

4. What does an author do?

5. What does an illustrator do?

6. Was this story written to teach us, or was it written to entertain us?

7. Is this story going to be fiction or nonfiction?

Part 3. Fiction: "A Trip to the Magic Sea" Shared Reading and Fluency Check

Gather the word cards that you cut out from page LC 83. Show them to students. Read the words aloud, pointing to each word as you read it.

Say: You will read aloud Part I and I will read aloud Part II. Then, you will read aloud Part III. These words will be in Parts I and III. Let's review the words together.

Reread the words, again pointing to each word as you read it aloud. Have students repeat each word several times.

Show the cards to students one at a time and ask students to read them.

- Circle any words that students read incorrectly.
- If students have trouble with a word, say, "This is the word [word]. Say [word]."

8. bored

9. Claire

10. story

11. paper airplane

12. finished

13. replied

You will use your copy of "A Trip to the Magic Sea" to note the kinds of errors that students make as they read. As you listen, you may choose to mark up your copy of the story where students have difficulty reading. Make a mark or a note for the following types of errors:

Listen for these types of errors	How many times?	Examples
Reads word incorrectly, does not self-correct.		
Skips a word, does not self-correct.		
Rereads before reading correctly.		
Guesses before reading correctly.		

Have students read aloud Part I. Students should read independently. As they read, mark on your copy any words they miss.

Read aloud Part II to students.

Have students read aloud Part III. Students should read independently. As they read, mark on your copy any words they miss.

Circle *Yes* or *No* for each question.

14. Did students read with a pace that sounds natural? Yes / No

15. Did students read with appropriate volume? Yes / No

16. Did students pause for periods? Yes / No

17. Did students read with expression? Yes / No

Part 4. Fiction: "A Trip to the Magic Sea" Evaluate Predictions

Read the predictions students wrote in Part 2. Tell students that predictions are neither right nor wrong; they are just the best guess you can make with the information you have. Ask students the following questions and note their responses on the Checkpoint pages.

18. What helped you make your prediction?

19. What else could help a reader make a prediction?

20. Was your prediction accurate?

Part 5. Fiction: "A Trip to the Magic Sea" Draw Conclusions

Explain to students that after reading the story, they have enough information to draw conclusions about what happens next in the story, even though the author did not write any more. Note their response on the Checkpoint pages.

21. What do you think Claire did with her paper airplanes?

Part 6. Fiction: "A Trip to the Magic Sea" Reading Comprehension

Read the questions on the Checkpoint pages to students. Students should write the answers themselves. If necessary, allow them to dictate their responses to you.

Part 7. Fiction: "A Trip to the Magic Sea" Show You Know

Give students crayons and the blank story cards that you cut out from page LC 89. Have students draw pictures of the main events of the story.

22. Draw pictures of the main events of the story.

When they have finished the drawings, students should give you the cards. Put the cards in the order in which the events happened in the story. If necessary, ask students to describe the events depicted in the drawings. Have students retell the story and check whether you have put the cards in the right order.

33. Retell the story using the story cards.

34. Are the cards in the right order?

Part 8. Nonfiction: "The Wright Brothers" Preview the Article

Show students "The Wright Brothers." Point to and read aloud the title of the article. Preview the article with students. Have students find the time line.

35. Point to the time line.

Point to the heading **Two Brothers with One Dream**. Explain that the bold print is used to call attention to the text. This is a heading, and it gives us clues about the next paragraph. Have students read the heading and make a prediction. Note their response on the Checkpoint pages.

36. Read the heading.

37. What do you think this article will be about?

Have students locate other headings in the text. As students point to a heading, read aloud that heading. Note students' responses on the Checkpoint pages.

38. Point to the headings.

39. Why are the headings in bold print?

40. What is the topic of this article?

Before reading "The Wright Brothers," go over Words to Know with students. Read aloud each word and have students repeat it. Ask students if they know what each word means.

- If students know a word's meaning, have them define it and use it in a sentence.
- If students don't know a word's meaning, read them the definition and discuss the word with them.

machine – a combination of parts that use force, motion, and energy to do work

Part 9. Nonfiction: "The Wright Brothers" Read Aloud – Main Idea and Supporting Details

Gather the graphic organizer on pages LC 98 and 99.

41. Write each heading from the article in one of the empty boxes. As you listen, write the main idea and one supporting detail in each empty box.

Begin to read aloud "The Wright Brothers." Have students sit next to you so that they can see the words while you read aloud the text. Emphasize the word *machine* when you come to it.

Pause after reading each section. Have students write the main idea and a supporting detail for each section. If necessary, allow them to dictate their responses to you.

Part 10. Nonfiction: "The Wright Brothers" Reading Comprehension

Read the questions and answer choices to students and note their responses on the Checkpoint pages. You may allow students to circle the answers.

Part 11. Poetry: "So High" Activate Prior Knowledge

Explain to students that they will read a poem with you. Ask students the following questions to activate prior knowledge. Note their responses on the Checkpoint pages.

46. What do you know about poems?

47. I've read a story and an article to you. What was their topic?

48. What do you think this poem will be about?

Part 12. Poetry: "So High" Shared Reading and Fluency Check

Gather the Checkpoint page with "So High." Cut out the two copies of the poem and give one to students. Read aloud the title of the poem, pointing to each word as you read. Then, have students read aloud the title of the poem, pointing to each word as they read aloud.

Explain to students that a lot of the words in the poem repeat and that they should listen carefully and follow along as you read.

You will use your copy of "So High" to note the kinds of errors that students make as they read.

As you listen, you may choose to mark up your copy of the poem where students have difficulty reading. Make a mark or a note for the following types of errors:

Listen for these types of errors	How many times?	Examples
Reads word incorrectly, does not self-correct.		
Skips a word, does not self-correct.		
Rereads before reading correctly.		
Guesses before reading correctly.		

Read aloud the first stanza.

Have students read aloud the second stanza. As students read, mark on your copy any words they miss.

Read aloud the third stanza.

Have students read aloud the fourth stanza. As students read, mark on your copy any words they miss.

Circle *Yes* or *No* for each question.

49. Did students read with a pace that sounds natural? Yes / No

50. Did students read with appropriate volume? Yes / No

51. Did students pause for periods? Yes / No

52. Did students read with expression? Yes / No

Part 13. Poetry: "So High" Summarizing

Have students summarize the poem.

53. What is the poem about?

Part 14. Poetry: "So High" Evaluate Predictions

Read the predictions students made in Part 13. Ask students the following questions and note their responses on the Checkpoint pages.

54. What helped you make your prediction?

55. Was your prediction accurate?

Part 15. Poetry: "So High" Reading Comprehension

Read the questions on the Checkpoint pages to students. Students should write the answers themselves. If necessary, allow them to dictate their responses to you.

Part 16. Poetry: "So High" Draw Conclusions

Ask students the following question and note their response on the Checkpoint pages.

61. What is the author writing about when she writes "you do not have feathers and no beak to open wide"?

Part 17. Poetry: "So High" Illustrations

Give students crayons. Discuss with students the author's use of imagery, such as "Your wings are long / And shine in the light and You do not have feathers / And no beak to open wide." If necessary, read the poem aloud and tell students to close their eyes and try to picture the airplane as they listen.

62. Draw a picture to go with the poem.

Mid-Semester Checkpoint
Shared Reading Comprehension
and Analysis

Learning Coach Copy
A Trip to the Magic Sea

by Missy Gimble

I.

Claire was bored. She had read books and made pictures. She had played outside. Now, she was sitting at the kitchen table. She put her head down on her arms and watched her dad make lunch.

"I'm bored, Dad," Claire said.

"Don't worry. We will go on a trip to the beach in a few days. You will have lots to do then," her dad said.

"But, our trip is still three days away," Claire said. "What can I do to have fun until then?" she asked.

Her dad put lunch on the table and sat down. Claire raised her head and started to eat. "Did I ever tell you about Shawn?" her dad asked.

"No," Claire replied.

"He was my best friend when I was a kid. Shawn was never bored. Let me tell you why," said her dad. He took a bite of his lunch and began his story.

II .

Shawn loved making paper airplanes. He made big planes and small ones. He made them out of all kinds of paper. He knew how to fold their wings in different ways. He did that to make them fly faster or slower. The best thing about Shawn's planes was that they really flew. They didn't just fly across a room. They flew to far-off places.

"Finished!" Shawn said as he folded his piece of paper one last time. He held up his paper airplane and smiled. "Where do I want to go today? I know. I want to go to the Magic Sea!" Shawn closed his eyes. He held on tightly to his paper plane. Then, he started to turn in a circle. Shawn turned around and around until his feet

LITERATURE & COMPREHENSION

lifted off the ground. When they touched back down, he wasn't standing on a hard floor. He was standing on sand. Shawn opened his eyes and looked around. He was on the beach of the Magic Sea!

Shawn put his plane on the sand and ran to the water. "I wonder if they'll be here today," he thought. Just then, he saw sea animals swimming toward him. A small green whale splashed its tail. A red shark smiled. Pink and green fish swam up to his feet.

"Hi, Shawn!" a striped starfish said. "We're glad you came back. What would you like to do today?"

"Let's go for a ride!" Shawn said. Then, he dove into the water and swam to the shark. Shawn grabbed the shark's tail and held on. The shark swam through waves. He jumped high out of the water. He dove low through sea grass. Then, he took Shawn back to the beach.

Next, Shawn swam with seals. He played with turtles. He raced crabs. But, the sun was starting to set. It was getting late. "I've had a lot of fun, but it's time for me to go home," Shawn said.

"We're glad you came to play. See you next time!" the animals said. They all smiled and waved at Shawn.

Shawn picked up his paper plane. He closed his eyes and held on to it tightly. Then, he started to turn in a circle. Shawn turned around and around until his feet lifted off the ground. When they touched back down, he wasn't standing on sand. He was standing on a hard floor. Shawn opened his eyes and looked around. He was back in his room.

"That was another great trip!" Shawn said. He put his paper plane on a shelf full of other planes. He brushed the sand off his feet and went downstairs for dinner.

III.

Claire's dad finished his story. He saw that Claire had finished all her lunch. She had pushed her chair back from the table. She wanted to leave the room. "Claire," he asked, "did my story bore you even more?"

"No, Dad," Claire said. "I want to leave the table, but not because I'm bored. I want to leave so I can go make paper airplanes!"

Student Copy

A Trip to the Magic Sea

by Missy Gimble

I.

Claire was bored. She had read books and made pictures. She had played outside. Now, she was sitting at the kitchen table. She put her head down on her arms and watched her dad make lunch.

"I'm bored, Dad," Claire said.

"Don't worry. We will go on a trip to the beach in a few days. You will have lots to do then," her dad said.

"But, our trip is still three days away," Claire said. "What can I do to have fun until then?" she asked.

Her dad put lunch on the table and sat down. Claire raised her head and started to eat. "Did I ever tell you about Shawn?" her dad asked.

"No," Claire replied.

"He was my best friend when I was a kid. Shawn was never bored. Let me tell you why," said her dad. He took a bite of his lunch and began his story.

II.

Shawn loved making paper airplanes. He made big planes and small ones. He made them out of all kinds of paper. He knew how to fold their wings in different ways. He did that to make them fly faster or slower. The best thing about Shawn's planes was that they really flew. They didn't just fly across a room. They flew to far-off places.

"Finished!" Shawn said as he folded his piece of paper one last time. He held up his paper airplane and smiled. "Where do I want to go today? I know. I want to go to the Magic Sea!" Shawn closed his eyes. He held on tightly to his paper plane. Then, he started to turn in a circle. Shawn turned around and around until his feet lifted off the ground. When they touched back down, he wasn't standing on a hard floor. He was standing on sand. Shawn opened his eyes and looked around. He was on the beach of the Magic Sea!

Shawn put his plane on the sand and ran to the water. "I wonder if they'll be here today," he thought. Just then, he saw sea animals swimming toward him. A small green whale splashed its tail. A red shark smiled. Pink and green fish swam up to his feet.

"Hi, Shawn!" a striped starfish said. "We're glad you came back. What would you like to do today?"

"Let's go for a ride!" Shawn said. Then, he dove into the water and swam to the shark. Shawn grabbed the shark's tail and held on. The shark swam through waves. He jumped high out of the water. He dove low through sea grass. Then, he took Shawn back to the beach.

Next, Shawn swam with seals. He played with turtles. He raced crabs. But, the sun was starting to set. It was getting late. "I've had a lot of fun, but it's time for me to go home," Shawn said.

"We're glad you came to play. See you next time!" the animals said. They all smiled and waved at Shawn.

Shawn picked up his paper plane. He closed his eyes and held on to it tightly. Then, he started to turn in a circle. Shawn turned around and around until his feet lifted off the ground. When they touched back down, he wasn't standing on sand. He was standing on a hard floor. Shawn opened his eyes and looked around. He was back in his room.

"That was another great trip!" Shawn said. He put his paper plane on a shelf full of other planes. He brushed the sand off his feet and went downstairs for dinner.

III.

Claire's dad finished his story. He saw that Claire had finished all her lunch. She had pushed her chair back from the table. She wanted to leave the room. "Claire," he asked, "did my story bore you even more?"

"No, Dad," Claire said. "I want to leave the table, but not because I'm bored. I want to leave so I can go make paper airplanes!"

Part 1. Fiction: "A Trip to the Magic Sea"
Activate Prior Knowledge

Get ready to read. Listen to the question, and say your answer.

1.

2.

Part 2. Fiction: "A Trip to the Magic Sea"
Book Walk

Do a Book Walk. Listen to the question, and say your answer.

3.

4.

5.

6.

7.

Part 3. Fiction: "A Trip to the Magic Sea"
Shared Reading and Fluency Check

Cut out the word cards. Read aloud each word.

Claire

replied

paper airplane

bored

story

finished

8.

9.

10.

11.

12.

13.

14. –17.

Part 4. Fiction: "A Trip to the Magic Sea"
Evaluate Predictions

Listen to the question, and say your answer.

18.

19.

20.

Part 5. Fiction: "A Trip to the Magic Sea"
Draw Conclusions

Listen to the question, and say your answer.

21.

LITERATURE & COMPREHENSION

Part 6. Fiction: "A Trip to the Magic Sea"
Reading Comprehension

Listen to the question, and write the answer.

22. Who are the characters in the story?

_____

_____

23. What is the setting for Dad and Claire's part
of the story?

_____

24. What is the setting for Shawn's part of the story?

_____

_____

25. Did Shawn really go to the Magic Sea?

_____

_____

26. How can readers tell whether Shawn really went to the Magic Sea?

_____

_____

27. Is this story fiction or nonfiction?

_____

28. Is this story realistic or fantasy?

_____

29. What was Claire's problem?

_____

30. How did Dad help Claire solve her problem?

_____

31. Read the sentence from the story. How do we know what Claire said?

"I'm bored, Dad," Claire said.

_____

Part 7. Fiction: "A Trip to the Magic Sea"
Show You Know

Cut out the cards. Draw pictures of the main events on them.
Retell the story.

32.

33.

34.

The Wright Brothers

By C.S. Rey

What do you see when you look up at the sky?
You might see the sun and clouds if it's daytime.
You might see the moon and stars if it's nighttime.
Some days, you might see birds and butterflies.
People have always seen these things in the sky.
But, when you look up at the sky, you might see
something else. You might see something that
people long ago never saw. You might see airplanes.

Two Brothers with One Dream

Wilbur Wright had a dream. He dreamed of
building the first airplane. His brother Orville
shared the same dream. Wilbur was born on
April 16, 1867. Orville was born on August 19,
1871. When they were young boys, their father
gave them a special toy. It was a toy helicopter.

Wilbur (left) and Orville (right) Wright

The boys loved their toy. They played with it all the time. They learned how it worked. Then, they built their own. From then on, they wanted to learn as much as they could about flying. As they grew older, they didn't just want to *learn* about flying. They wanted to fly. But, how could they fly when no one had built an airplane yet? Wilbur and Orville had a plan to solve their problem. They planned to build the first airplane. They knew it would be hard work. But, they didn't let that stop them.

Learning from Others

The Wright brothers were not the first people to try to build an airplane. Other people had tried, too. Wilbur and Orville learned from those people. They read all about the machines those people had built. They looked at pictures of the machines. They learned why those machines didn't work. The Wright brothers learned a lot. They used what they learned to help build their plane.

Learning from Birds

The Wright brothers knew they had to be able to steer their airplane. They had to be able to steer it on the ground and once it was in the air. But, they didn't know how to make their plane turn from side to side. None of the machines they had studied could turn safely. The brothers knew how to solve their problem. They looked for help somewhere else. This time, they didn't learn from other people. They didn't learn from machines. They learned from birds.

Wilbur and Orville watched birds as they flew. They saw the birds use their wings to turn. They learned that birds raise and lower parts of their wings to turn from side to side. The Wright brothers used what they learned from birds to help build their plane.

Up, Up, and Away!

Wilbur and Orville spent years learning from other people and from birds. They learned from their own machines, too. They built their first flying machine in 1899. Their machine didn't look the way planes look today. It was small. It was just 5 feet wide. That's about how wide a small car is today. Their first machine didn't have a motor. No one sat on the machine to fly it. The brothers flew it like a kite. They stood on the ground and held ropes that moved the wings.

The Wright brothers spent the next four years building new machines. They tested each one. They learned what worked on each machine. They learned what didn't work, too. They used what they learned to make each machine better.

They built their machines bigger and bigger. They flew the first ones from the ground like kites. Then, they started riding in the machines to fly them. But none of their machines had motors. They all needed wind to fly.

In 1903, the Wright brothers built a new machine. They called it the *Wright Flyer I*. This machine was not like their others. It was their first one with a motor. On December 17, 1903, the brothers were ready to test their airplane. Orville flew their plane the first time. He flew it for 12 seconds. Then, the brothers took turns flying their plane. They flew it three more times that day. None of their flights lasted a long time. They were all less than a minute. But, their four short flights were all it took. The Wright brothers proved people could fly!

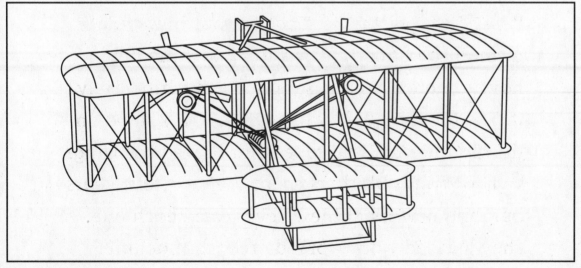

The *Wright Flyer I*

LITERATURE & COMPREHENSION

The World's First Pilots

| **April 16, 1867** Wilbur Wright is born. | **August 19, 1871** Orville Wright is born. | **1899** Wilbur and Orville Wright build their first flying machine. **1903** Wilbur and Orville Wright build the *Wright Flyer I.* | **December 17, 1903** Orville Wright becomes the first person to fly an airplane. |

LITERATURE & COMPREHENSION

Part 8. Nonfiction: "The Wright Brothers"
Preview the Article

Listen to the question, and say your answer.

35.

36.

37.

38.

39.

40.

Part 9. Nonfiction: "The Wright Brothers"
Read Aloud — Main Idea and Supporting Details

Write each heading. Listen to the article, and write the main idea and one supporting detail for each section.

41.

	First section	Second section
Heading		
Main idea		
Supporting detail		

	Third section	**Fourth section**
Heading		
Main idea		
Supporting detail		

Part 10. Nonfiction: "The Wright Brothers" Reading Comprehension

Listen to the question, and choose the answer.

42. What did the Wright brothers build?

    A. a toy submarine

    B. an airplane

    C. model birds

43. What did the Wright brothers learn from birds?

    A. how to land

    B. how to take off

    C. how to steer

44. When did the Wright brothers build their first flying machine?

    A. 1899   B. 1903   C. 1939

45. How long did the Wright brothers' first flight last?

    A. 12 hours

    B. 12 minutes

    C. 12 seconds

Student Copy

So High

I stand on the ground
And look up to the sky
I watch you fly
So high, so high

Your wings are long
And shine in the light
I watch you fly
So high, so high

You do not have feathers
And no beak to open wide
I watch you fly
So high, so high

I stand on the ground
And look up to the sky
I watch the airplane fly
So high, so high

Learning Coach Copy

So High

I stand on the ground
And look up to the sky
I watch you fly
So high, so high

Your wings are long
And shine in the light
I watch you fly
So high, so high

You do not have feathers
And no beak to open wide
I watch you fly
So high, so high

I stand on the ground
And look up to the sky
I watch the airplane fly
So high, so high

Part 11. Poetry: "So High" Activate Prior Knowledge

Get ready to read. Listen to the question, and say your answer.

46.

47.

48.

Part 12. Poetry: "So High" Shared Reading and Fluency Check

Read aloud the poem.

49.–52.

LITERATURE & COMPREHENSION

LITERATURE & COMPREHENSION

Part 13. Poetry: "So High" Summarizing
Listen to the question, and say your answer.

53.

Part 14. Poetry: "So High" Evaluate Predictions
Listen to the question, and say your answer.

54.

55.

Part 15. Poetry: "So High" Reading Comprehension

Listen to the question, and write the answer.

56. What is the topic of "So High"?

_____

57. What do the words *so high, so high* make you feel like?

_____

_____

58. Which words repeat throughout the poem?

_____

_____

59. Why does the author repeat those words?

_____

_____

60. Which words rhyme in the poem?

_____

Part 16. Poetry: "So High" Draw Conclusions
Listen to the question, and say your answer.

61.

Part 17. Poetry: "So High" Illustration
Draw a picture to go with the poem.

62.

Semester Checkpoint
Learning Coach Instructions
Guided Reading Comprehension
and Analysis

Explain that students are going to show what they have learned this semester.

- Give students pages LC 115–LC 160 of the Semester Checkpoint.
- Read the directions on the students' pages together. Use the Learning Coach instructions on pages LC 107–LC 114 to administer the Checkpoint.
- Use the Checkpoint pages to record student behaviors and responses.
- When you have finished, use the Answer Key to score the Checkpoint and then enter the results online.
- Review each exercise with students. Work with students to correct any exercise that they missed.

Part 1. Fiction: "Bad Dog, Chester!" Activate Prior Knowledge

Ask students the following questions to activate prior knowledge. Note their responses on the Checkpoint pages.

1. What do you know about dogs?

2. What are some things pets can do to get in trouble?

Before students read "Bad Dog, Chester!" go over Words to Know with students. Read aloud each word and have students repeat it. Ask students if they know what each word means.

- If students know a word's meaning, have them define it and use it in a sentence.
- If students don't know a word's meaning, read them the definition and discuss the word with them.

glance – to look at something quickly
perch – a bar or branch on which a bird can sit
ruined – destroyed or spoiled

Part 2. Fiction: "Bad Dog, Chester!" Book Walk

Gather the Checkpoint pages with "Bad Dog, Chester!" Note that there are two versions of the story: One is the full story for the students, and the other is a copy for you to follow and mark as students read aloud. Have students sit next to you so that they can see the story while you do a Book Walk. Read aloud the title and author of the text. Show students the illustration. Ask students the following questions and have them write their responses on the Checkpoint pages. If necessary, allow them to dictate their responses to you.

3. Was this story written to teach us, or was it written to entertain us?

4. Is this story going to be fiction or nonfiction?

Part 3. Fiction: "Bad Dog, Chester!" Guided Reading and Fluency Check

Gather the word cards from page LC 125. Show them to students. Read aloud the words, pointing to each word as you read it. Reread the words, again pointing to each word as you read it aloud. Have students repeat each word several times. Show the cards to students, one card at a time, and ask students to read them.

- Circle any words that students read incorrectly.
- If students have trouble with a word, say, "This is the word [word]. Say [word]."

5. furniture

6. glance

7. ruined

8. perch

9. curtains

Say: You will read aloud the story to me. If you would like to read the story to yourself first, you may.

Use your copy of "Bad Dog, Chester!" to note the kinds of errors that students make as they read. As you listen, you may choose to mark up your copy of the story where students have difficulty reading. Make a mark or a note for the following types of errors:

Listen for these types of errors	How many times?	Examples
Reads word incorrectly, does not self-correct.		
Skips a word, does not self-correct.		
Rereads before reading correctly.		
Guesses before reading correctly.		

Have students read aloud the story. Students should read independently. As students read, mark on your copy any words they miss.

Circle *Yes* or *No* for each question.

10. Did students read with a pace that sounds natural? Yes / No

11. Did students read with appropriate volume? Yes / No

12. Did students pause for periods? Yes / No

13. Did students read with expression? Yes / No

Part 4. Fiction: "Bad Dog, Chester!" Evaluate Predictions

Read the prediction students wrote in Part 2. Tell students that predictions are neither right nor wrong; they are just the best guess you can make with the information you have. Ask students the following questions and have students write their responses on the Checkpoint pages. If necessary, allow them to dictate their responses to you.

14. What helped you make your prediction?

15. What else could help a reader make a prediction?

16. Was your prediction accurate?

Part 5. Fiction: "Bad Dog, Chester!" Problem and Solution

Explain to students that during the story, Chester has a problem that needs to be solved. Ask students the following questions and have them write their responses on the Checkpoint pages. If necessary, allow them to dictate their responses to you.

17. What is Chester's problem in this story?

18. What is a solution?

19. How does Chester solve his problem?

Part 6. Fiction: "Bad Dog, Chester!" Reading Comprehension

Read the questions on the Checkpoint pages to students. Students should write their responses. If necessary, allow them to dictate their responses to you.

Part 7. Fiction: "Bad Dog, Chester!" Show You Know

Turn to the graphic organizer on page LC 131. Before students complete the graphic organizer, ask the following questions. Note students' responses on the Checkpoint pages.

25. Who is telling the story in "Bad Dog, Chester!"?

26. What happens first in the story?

27. What happens next?

28. What happens last?

Have students complete the graphic organizer independently. Students should be able to identify the title, characters, setting, problem, and solution. Additionally, they should write a brief plot summary of the story. If necessary, allow them to dictate their responses to you.

29.–34. Complete the graphic organizer.

Part 8. Nonfiction: "The First Chimp in Space" Preview the Article

Gather the Checkpoint pages with "The First Chimp in Space." Have students sit next to you so that they can see the story while you preview the article. Show students "The First Chimp in Space." Point to and read aloud the title of the article. Preview the article with students.

35. What do you think will be the topic of this article?

Point to the heading **Learning from Animals**. Explain that the bold print is used to call attention to the text. This is a heading, and it gives us clues about the next paragraph. Have students read the heading and make a prediction. Note their response on the Checkpoint pages.

36. Read the first heading.

37. What do you think this section will be about?

Have students locate and read aloud the other headings in the text and make a prediction about each section. Note students' responses on the Checkpoint pages.

38. Read the second heading.

39. What do you think this section will be about?

40. Read the third heading.

41. What do you think this section will be about?

42. Read the fourth heading.

43. What do you think this section will be about?

Part 9. Nonfiction: "The First Chimp in Space" Guided Reading and Fluency Check

Before students read "The First Chimp in Space," go over Words to Know with students. Read aloud each word and have students repeat it. Ask students if they know what each word means.

- If students know a word's meaning, have them define it and use it in a sentence.
- If students don't know a word's meaning, read them the definition and discuss the word with them.

LITERATURE & COMPREHENSION

complete – finish

lever – a bar or handle used to work a machine

international – involving different countries

Gather the word cards from pages LC 143 and 145. Show them to students. Read the words aloud, pointing to each word as you read it. Reread the words, again pointing to each word as you read it aloud. Have students repeat each word several times. Show the cards to students, one card at a time, and ask students to read them.

- Circle any words that students read incorrectly.
- If students have trouble with a word, say, "This is the word [*word*]. Say [*word*]."

44. scientist

45. machine

46. chimpanzee

47. complete

48. lever

49. international

50. mission

Say: You will read aloud the article to me. If you would like to read the article to yourself first, you may.

Use your copy of "The First Chimp in Space" to note the kinds of errors that students make as they read. As you listen, you may choose to mark up your copy of the story where students have difficulty reading. Make a mark or a note for the following types of errors:

Listen for these types of errors	How many times?	Examples
Reads word incorrectly, does not self-correct.		
Skips a word, does not self-correct.		
Rereads before reading correctly.		
Guesses before reading correctly.		

Sidebar: LITERATURE & COMPREHENSION

Have students read aloud the article. Students should read independently. As students read, mark on your copy any words they miss.

Circle *Yes* or *No* for each question.

51. Did students read with a pace that sounds natural? Yes / No

52. Did students read with appropriate volume? Yes / No

53. Did students pause for periods? Yes / No

54. Did students read with expression? Yes / No

Part 10. Nonfiction: "The First Chimp in Space" Create a Time Line

Gather the time line boxes on page LC 149. Have students fill in the six major events in Ham's life. Then have them paste the events on the time line on page LC 151 in the order that they happened.

55.–60. Complete the time line.

Part 11. Nonfiction: "The First Chimp in Space" Reading Comprehension

Have students read and answer the questions on the Checkpoint pages. Students should circle their answers.

Part 12. Poetry: "My Day" Activate Prior Knowledge

Explain to students that they will read a poem with you. Ask students the following questions to activate prior knowledge. Note their responses on the Checkpoint pages.

66. What do you know about poems?

67. You've read a story and an article. What are they mostly about? What kind of characters do they have?

68. What do you think this poem will be about?

Part 13. Poetry: "My Day" Guided Reading and Fluency Check

Gather the Checkpoint page with "My Day." Cut out the two copies of the poem and give one to students. Read aloud the title of the poem, pointing to each word as you read. Then, have students read aloud the title of the poem, pointing to each word as they read aloud.

Say: You will read aloud the poem to me. If you would like to read the poem to yourself first, you may.

Use your copy of "My Day" to note the kinds of errors that students make as they read.

As you listen, you may choose to mark up your copy of the poem where students have difficulty reading. Make a mark or a note for the following types of errors:

Listen for these types of errors	How many times?	Examples
Reads word incorrectly, does not self-correct.		
Skips a word, does not self-correct.		
Rereads before reading correctly.		
Guesses before reading correctly.		

Have students read aloud the poem. Students should read independently. As students read, mark on your copy any words they miss.

Circle *Yes* or *No* for each question.

69. Did students read with a pace that sounds natural? Yes / No

70. Did students read with appropriate volume? Yes / No

71. Did students pause for periods? Yes / No

72. Did students read with expression? Yes / No

Part 14. Poetry: "My Day" Draw Conclusions

Have students draw conclusions about the poem. Ask students the following questions and note their responses on the Checkpoint pages.

73. What is the poem about?

74. What lines from the poem helped you figure out what the poem is about?

Part 15. Poetry: "My Day" Reading Comprehension

Read the questions on the Checkpoint pages to students. Students should write the answers themselves. If necessary, allow them to dictate their responses to you.

Part 16. Poetry: "My Day" Write Your Own Poem

Turn to the poetry frame on page LC 160. Have students complete the poem independently. Students should use words from the word bank to complete the poem using the same rhyming pattern as the author used in "My Day." If necessary, allow them to dictate their responses to you.

Semester Checkpoint
Guided Reading Comprehension
and Analysis

Learning Coach Copy
Bad Dog, Chester!

by Missy Tisch

Every day I hear the same thing: "Bad dog, Chester!" Some days I hear it as soon as I wake up. Some days I hear it after lunch. Some days I hear it at bedtime. But, I'm not a bad dog. You might not believe me, but it's true. I know all my commands. I never jump up on people. I don't beg for food. I'm a good dog. I know what you're wondering. If I'm such a good dog, then why do I hear "Bad dog, Chester!" every day? I'll tell you why. Gabby.

Gabby is the bird. Since she moved in, life has never been the same. Gabby has a cage, but the door is always open. She gets to fly all over the house. Most people think she's the perfect bird. But, they don't see the Gabby that I see. Gabby is the one that knocked over the vase of flowers. Gabby is the one that ruined the curtains. Gabby is the one that got the furniture dirty. But, Gabby doesn't hear "Bad bird, Gabby!" Do you know why? Because after Gabby does something bad, she flies into her cage. She sits on her perch,

chirping like the perfect bird. So, what happens when people find her messes? I get blamed for them!

But, not today. I've come up with a plan. I just need to watch Gabby closely. As soon as she starts to cause trouble, I know just what I'll do. There she goes! Gabby is flying near the fresh pie cooling on the table. She's going to try to take a bite. Now's my chance!

"Woof! Woof!" I bark.

"What is it, Chester? Why are you scratching at the door? Is it time for your walk?" Kate asks.

"Woof!" I reply.

Kate grabs my leash and we head out the door. I glance back at Gabby. She hasn't even noticed I left the room.

When Kate and I get back from our walk, the kitchen is a mess. Pie is everywhere. Pie is on the table. Pie is on the floor. Pie is on the chairs. I look at Kate. She's not happy. She looks at me, and I can see that she knows the truth now.

"Bad bird, Gabby!" Kate says. "Good boy, Chester. I'm sorry I blamed you for everything."

That's all I needed to hear. I give Kate a big lick on the face and help her clean up the kitchen. After all, fresh pie is my favorite!

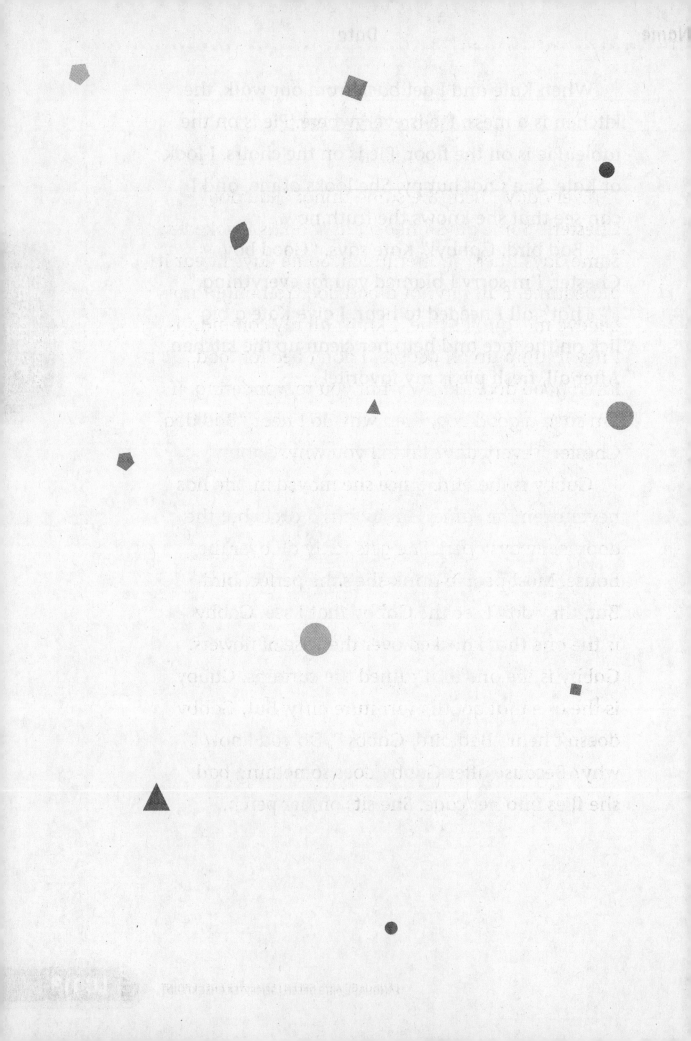

Student Copy
Bad Dog, Chester!
by Missy Tisch

Every day I hear the same thing: "Bad dog, Chester!" Some days I hear it as soon as I wake up. Some days I hear it after lunch. Some days I hear it at bedtime. But, I'm not a bad dog. You might not believe me, but it's true. I know all my commands. I never jump up on people. I don't beg for food. I'm a good dog. I know what you're wondering. If I'm such a good dog, then why do I hear "Bad dog, Chester!" every day? I'll tell you why. Gabby.

Gabby is the bird. Since she moved in, life has never been the same. Gabby has a cage, but the door is always open. She gets to fly all over the house. Most people think she's the perfect bird. But, they don't see the Gabby that I see. Gabby is the one that knocked over the vase of flowers. Gabby is the one that ruined the curtains. Gabby is the one that got the furniture dirty. But, Gabby doesn't hear "Bad bird, Gabby!" Do you know why? Because after Gabby does something bad, she flies into her cage. She sits on her perch,

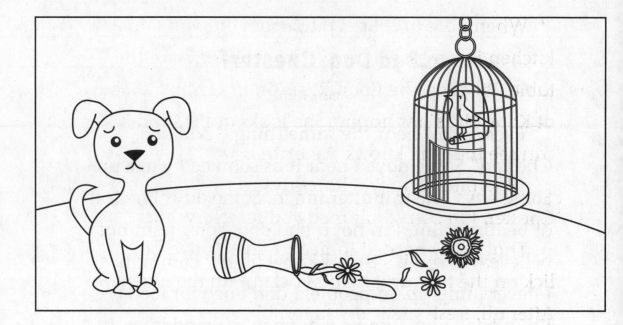

chirping like the perfect bird. So, what happens when people find her messes? I get blamed for them!

But, not today. I've come up with a plan. I just need to watch Gabby closely. As soon as she starts to cause trouble, I know just what I'll do. There she goes! Gabby is flying near the fresh pie cooling on the table. She's going to try to take a bite. Now's my chance!

"Woof! Woof!" I bark.

"What is it, Chester? Why are you scratching at the door? Is it time for your walk?" Kate asks.

"Woof!" I reply.

Kate grabs my leash and we head out the door. I glance back at Gabby. She hasn't even noticed I left the room.

When Kate and I get back from our walk, the kitchen is a mess. Pie is everywhere. Pie is on the table. Pie is on the floor. Pie is on the chairs. I look at Kate. She's not happy. She looks at me, and I can see that she knows the truth now.

"Bad bird, Gabby!" Kate says. "Good boy, Chester. I'm sorry I blamed you for everything."

That's all I needed to hear. I give Kate a big lick on the face and help her clean up the kitchen. After all, fresh pie is my favorite!

Part 1. Fiction: "Bad Dog, Chester!"
Activate Prior Knowledge

Get ready to read. Listen to the question, and say the answer.

1.

2.

Part 2. Fiction: "Bad Dog, Chester!"
Book Walk

Do a Book Walk. Listen to the question, and write the answer.

3. _____

4. _____

Part 3. Fiction: "Bad Dog, Chester!"
Guided Reading and Fluency Check

Cut out the word cards. Read aloud each word.

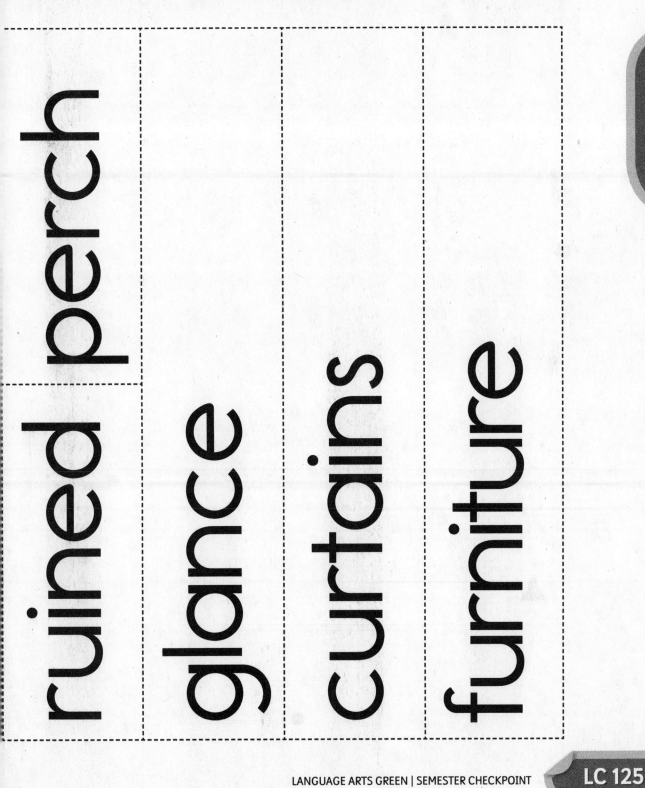

ruined

perch

glance

curtains

furniture

5.

6.

7.

8.

9.

10.–13.

Part 4. Fiction: "Bad Dog, Chester!"
Evaluate Predictions

Listen to the question, and write the answer.

14. _____

_____

15. _____

_____

16. _____

_____

Part 5. "Bad Dog, Chester!" Problem and Solution

Listen to the question, and write the answer.

17. _____

_____

18. _____

19. _____

_____

Part 6. Fiction: "Bad Dog, Chester!"
Reading Comprehension

Listen to the question, and write the answer.

20. Who is narrating the story?

_____

_____

21. What is the setting?

_____

_____

22. What are some examples of cause and effect in this story?

_____

_____

_____

_____

23. Is this story realistic fiction or fantasy fiction?

_____

24. How do you know?

_____

_____

Part 7. Fiction: "Bad Dog, Chester!" Show You Know

Listen to the question, and say the answer. Then, complete the graphic organizer.

25.

26.

27.

28.

29.–34.

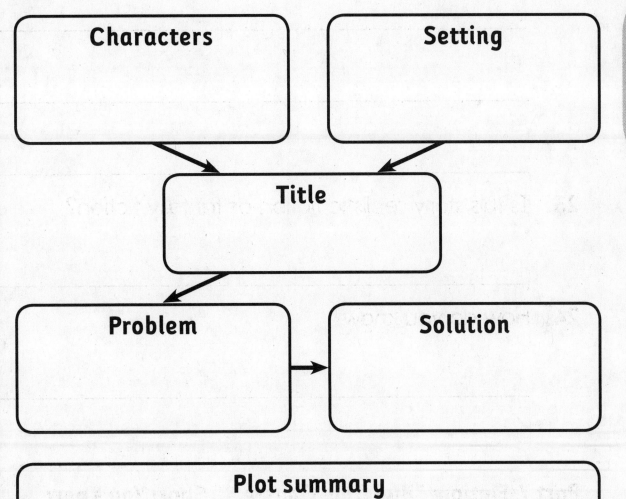

Characters

Setting

Title

Problem

Solution

Plot summary

The First Chimp in Space

by Maude Drayber

Chimpanzees are smart animals. They can be trained to do a lot of things. One chimp was trained for a very special job. His name was Ham. Ham's job wasn't on earth. His job was in space!

Learning from Animals

The first rockets to fly to space didn't carry people. They carried animals. Some carried mice. Some carried dogs. Other kinds of animals flew to space, too. Scientists learned from the animals. They learned it was safe to fly to space. But, they wanted to know more. They wanted to know if astronauts would be able to complete tasks in space. They decided to send a chimp to space to find out. They chose Ham.

Training for the Big Day

Ham was born in 1957. In 1959, he began training for his space flight. Ham learned a lot of things. He learned to wear a special suit. He learned how it would feel to ride in a rocket. Ham had to learn a job, too. He learned how to push a lever when he saw a light flash. He was good at his job. Scientists knew Ham could do his job on earth. They hoped he could do it in space, too.

3 . . . 2 . . . 1 . . . Blast Off!

January 31, 1961, was Ham's big day. That was the day he flew to space. Scientists got Ham ready for his flight. They fed him. They got him dressed. They hooked him up to machines. The machines let them see how Ham was feeling during his flight. They could see how fast or slow Ham was breathing. They could see how fast or slow his heart was beating. The machines let them know if Ham was safe.

Scientists wanted to know more than how Ham felt during his flight. They wanted to know if he could do his job, too. When it was time, the light in the rocket flashed for Ham. Would Ham push the lever? Scientists didn't have to wait long to find out. Ham pushed the lever almost as fast as he pushed it on earth. The scientists were thrilled! Ham had done more than just ride in a rocket. He had proved it was possible to complete tasks in space.

Ham the chimp in his special seat for the flight

After the Mission

Ham flew to space just one time. His flight was short. It was less than 17 minutes long. But, his flight was more important than the flights of all the other animals.

In 1963, Ham went to live at the National Zoo. It is a famous zoo in Washington, D.C. He lived there for a long time. In 1980, Ham moved. He went to live at the North Carolina Zoo. It was his home for the rest of his life. He died there in 1983. Ham is buried at a special place. He is buried at the International Space Hall of Fame. The Hall of Fame is in New Mexico. A lot of people go to see Ham's grave each year. They go to learn more about his special flight. And, they go to thank the most important chimp of all time.

The First Chimp in Space

by Maude Drayber

Chimpanzees are smart animals. They can be trained to do a lot of things. One chimp was trained for a very special job. His name was Ham. Ham's job wasn't on earth. His job was in space!

Learning from Animals

The first rockets to fly to space didn't carry people. They carried animals. Some carried mice. Some carried dogs. Other kinds of animals flew to space, too. Scientists learned from the animals. They learned it was safe to fly to space. But, they wanted to know more. They wanted to know if astronauts would be able to complete tasks in space. They decided to send a chimp to space to find out. They chose Ham.

Training for the Big Day

Ham was born in 1957. In 1959, he began training for his space flight. Ham learned a lot of things. He learned to wear a special suit. He learned how it would feel to ride in a rocket. Ham had to learn a job, too. He learned how to push a lever when he saw a light flash. He was good at his job. Scientists knew Ham could do his job on earth. They hoped he could do it in space, too.

LITERATURE & COMPREHENSION

3 . . . 2 . . . 1 . . . Blast Off!

January 31, 1961, was Ham's big day. That was the day he flew to space. Scientists got Ham ready for his flight. They fed him. They got him dressed. They hooked him up to machines. The machines let them see how Ham was feeling during his flight. They could see how fast or slow Ham was breathing. They could see how fast or slow his heart was beating. The machines let them know if Ham was safe.

Scientists wanted to know more than how Ham felt during his flight. They wanted to know if he could do his job, too. When it was time, the light in the rocket flashed for Ham. Would Ham push the lever? Scientists didn't have to wait long to find out. Ham pushed the lever almost as fast as he pushed it on earth. The scientists were thrilled! Ham had done more than just ride in a rocket. He had proved it was possible to complete tasks in space.

Ham the chimp in his special seat for the flight

LITERATURE & COMPREHENSION

After the Mission

Ham flew to space just one time. His flight was short. It was less than 17 minutes long. But, his flight was more important than the flights of all the other animals.

In 1963, Ham went to live at the National Zoo. It is a famous zoo in Washington, D.C. He lived there for a long time. In 1980, Ham moved. He went to live at the North Carolina Zoo. It was his home for the rest of his life. He died there in 1983. Ham is buried at a special place. He is buried at the International Space Hall of Fame. The Hall of Fame is in New Mexico. A lot of people go to see Ham's grave each year. They go to learn more about his special flight. And, they go to thank the most important chimp of all time.

Part 8. Nonfiction: "The First Chimp in Space"
Preview the Article

Listen to the question, and say your answer.

35.

36.

37.

38.

39.

40.

41.

42.

43.

Part 9. Nonfiction: "The First Chimp in Space"
Guided Reading and Fluency Check

Cut out the word cards. Read aloud each word.

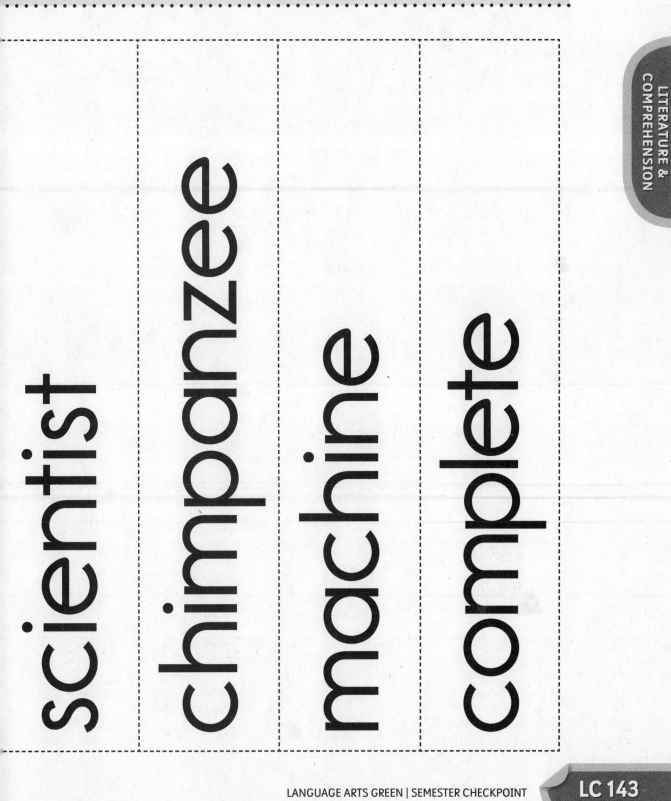

scientist

chimpanzee

machine

complete

LITERATURE & COMPREHENSION

international

mission

lever

44.

45.

46.

47.

48.

49.

50.

51.–54.

Part 10. Nonfiction: "The First Chimp in Space"
Create a Time Line

Write the year and the six major events from Ham's life in each box. Then, cut out the events, and paste them on the time line in the order that they happened.

55.–60.

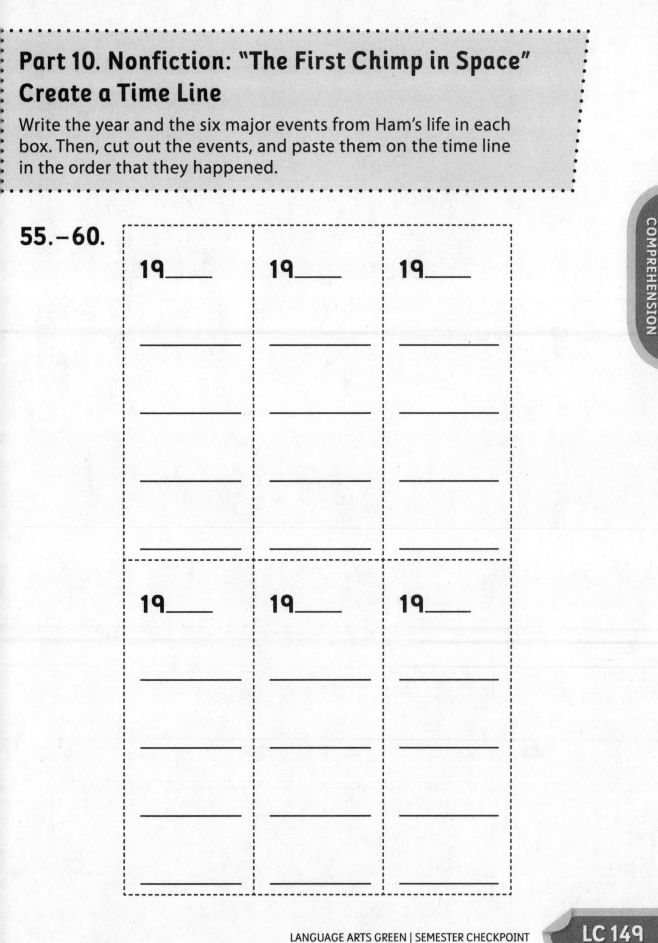

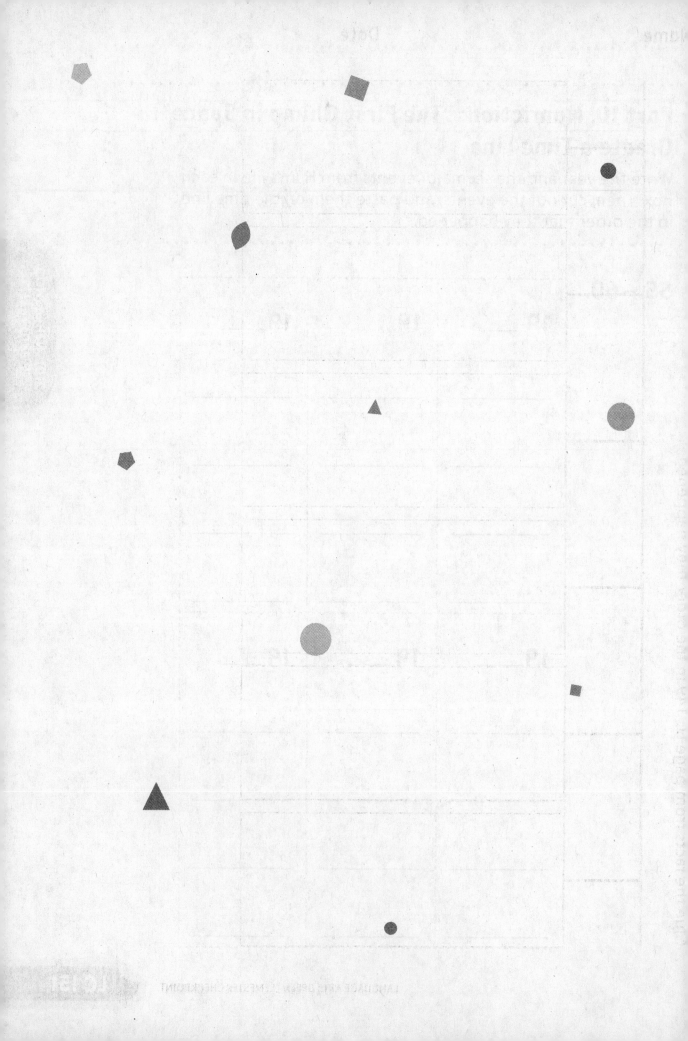

Glue the facts from page LC 149 in the order they happened.

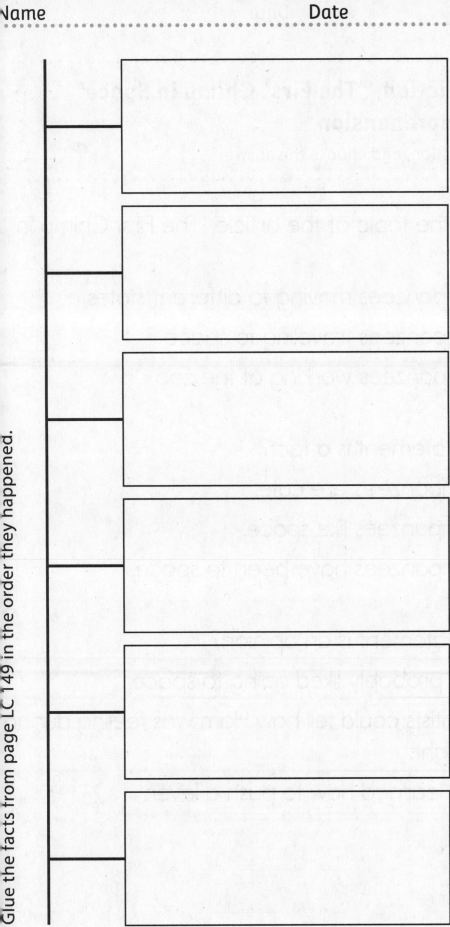

Part 11. Nonfiction: "The First Chimp in Space" Reading Comprehension

Listen to the question, and choose the answer.

61. What is the topic of the article "The First Chimp in Space"?

   A. chimpanzees moving to different states

   B. chimpanzees traveling to space

   C. chimpanzees working at the zoo

62. Which statement is a fact?

   A. Chimpanzees are cute.

   B. Chimpanzees like space.

   C. Chimpanzees have been to space.

63. Which statement is an opinion?

   A. Ham probably liked going to space.

   B. Scientists could tell how Ham was feeling during his flight.

   C. Ham learned how to push a lever.

64. What did Ham learn first?

    A. how to ride in a rocket

    B. how to do a job

    C. how to wear a special suit

65. If you wanted to learn more about Ham, what would be a good source of information?

    A. a cartoon about chimps traveling in space

    B. a book of facts about Ham and other animals that have worked in space

    C. a story a friend told you about chimps working and traveling

Student Copy

My Day

Alone in our big house,
I look for a small mouse.
When I don't find my tasty snack,
I purr and nap on my striped back.

Alone in the long and quiet hall,
I watch shadows dance on the white wall.
When they chase me through the big door,
I roll with them on the soft floor.

Alone on your cozy bed,
I stretch and rest my tired head.
When you climb under the cool sheet,
I curl up next to your warm feet.

Learning Coach Copy

My Day

Alone in our big house,
I look for a small mouse.
When I don't find my tasty snack,
I purr and nap on my striped back.

Alone in the long and quiet hall,
I watch shadows dance on the white wall.
When they chase me through the big door,
I roll with them on the soft floor.

Alone on your cozy bed,
I stretch and rest my tired head.
When you climb under the cool sheet,
I curl up next to your warm feet.

Part 12. Poetry: "My Day"
Activate Prior Knowledge

Get ready to read. Listen to the question, and say the answer.

66.

67.

68.

Part 13. Poetry: "My Day"
Guided Reading and Fluency Check

Read aloud the poem.

69.–72.

Part 14. Poetry: "My Day" Draw Conclusions

Listen to the question, and say the answer.

73.

74.

Part 15. Poetry: "My Day"
Reading Comprehension

Listen to the question, and write the answer.

75. What is the topic of "My Day"?

_____

76. What is the rhyming pattern in "My Day"?

_____

_____

77. What words rhyme in the poem "My Day"?

_____

_____

78. Reread the first stanza. What descriptive words did the author use?

_____

_____

79. Reread the second stanza. What is something the poet gave human qualities to?

_____

_____

_____

LITERATURE & COMPREHENSION

Part 16. Poetry: "My Day" Write Your Own Poem

Think about a pet you have or would like to have. Using the same rhyming pattern as the author used in "My Day," complete the poem.

80. Use words from the following list to complete the poem.

walk	talk	beets
squawk	treats	sweets
fly	cry	sigh

My Favorite Pet

My favorite pet loves to _____.

But the poor little thing can't _____.

My favorite pet loves to eat _____.

But I don't give my pet _____.

I take care of my pet every day.
I hope my pet never goes away.

Writing Skills

Unit Checkpoint Learning Coach Instructions
Complete Sentences

Explain that students are going to show what they have learned about recognizing and writing complete sentences with correct capitalization and end marks.

1. Give students the Unit Checkpoint pages.

2. Read the directions together. If needed, read the questions and answer choices to students. Have students complete the Checkpoint on their own.

3. Use the Answer Key to score the Checkpoint and then enter the results online.

4. Review each exercise with students. Work with students to correct any exercise that they missed.

Unit Checkpoint
Complete Sentences

Part 1. Complete Sentences
Choose the complete sentence.

1. Which is the complete sentence?

    A. Walks to the park.

    B. My sister.

    C. We all walk to the park.

2. Which is the complete sentence?

    A. Dogs and cats chase bugs.

    B. The many pets in the park.

    C. Ran around the trees and flowers.

3. Which is the complete sentence?

    A. He sat.

    B. Played in the grass.

    C. My friend and I.

4. Which is the complete sentence?

    A. Saw a mouse.

    B. The mouse went into a hole.

    C. My sisters Beth and Lisa.

Part 2. Sentence Beginnings and Endings
Choose the sentence that begins and ends correctly.

5. Which sentence begins and ends correctly?

    A. We played checkers.

    B. we played checkers

    C. we played checkers.

6. Which sentence begins and ends correctly?

    A. my brother won.

    B. My brother won.

    C. My brother won

7. Which sentence begins and ends correctly?

    A. He watched a movie

    B. he watched a movie

    C. He watched a movie.

WRITING SKILLS

Part 3. Identify the Naming Part

Draw one line under the naming part of the sentence.

8. The crab crawls in the sand.

9. We drive to the beach.

Part 4. Identify the Action Part

Draw two lines under the action part of the sentence.

10. My dog and I swim.

11. I look at the fish.

Part 5. Write a Complete Sentence

Write a sentence that begins and ends correctly.

12. _____

_____

Unit Checkpoint Learning Coach Instructions
Kinds of Sentences

Explain that students are going to show what they have learned about recognizing different kinds of sentences and capitalizing and punctuating them correctly.

1. Give students the Unit Checkpoint pages.

2. Read the directions together. If needed, read the questions and answer choices to students. Have students complete the Checkpoint on their own.

3. Use the Answer Key to score the Checkpoint and then enter the results online.

4. Review each exercise with students. Work with students to correct any exercise that they missed.

Unit Checkpoint Answer Key
Kinds of Sentences

> ## Part 1. Statement, Command, Question, or Exclamation
> Read the sentence. Choose what kind of sentence it is.

1. The snow falls.
   - **A.** command
   - **B.** statement
   - **C.** question
   - **D.** exclamation

2. It is freezing outside!
   - **A.** command
   - **B.** statement
   - **C.** question
   - **D.** exclamation

3. Where are your mittens?
   - **A.** command
   - **B.** statement
   - **C.** question
   - **D.** exclamation

4. Put your hat on.
   - **A.** command
   - **B.** statement
   - **C.** question
   - **D.** exclamation

Part 2. Choose the End Mark

Choose the end mark that belongs at the end of the sentence.

5. Exclamation: Today is my birthday

    A. .

    B. !

    C. ?

6. Statement: I am six years old

    A. !

    B. ?

    C. .

7. Command: Give me a gift, please

    A. .

    B. !

    C. ?

8. Question: Is that present mine

    A. ?

    B. .

    C. !

Part 3. Fix This Sentence

Write the sentence on the line. Be sure that it begins and ends correctly.

9. which bus should we take

_____

_____

10. we need to take the bus to town

_____

_____

11. there it is

_____

_____

WRITING SKILLS

Unit Checkpoint Learning Coach Instructions
Nouns

Explain that students are going to show what they have learned about identifying and using common, proper, and possessive nouns.

1. Give students the Unit Checkpoint pages.

2. Read the directions together. If needed, read the questions and answer choices to students. Have students complete the Checkpoint on their own.

3. Use the Answer Key to score the Checkpoint and then enter the results online.

4. Review each exercise with students. Work with students to correct any exercise that they missed.

Unit Checkpoint
Nouns

Part 1. Identify Nouns
Read the sentence. Choose the word that is a noun.

1. This is Fred.

   A. This   **B.** is   **C.** Fred

2. He is a big parrot.

   A. is   **B.** big   **C.** parrot

3. His feathers are beautiful.

   A. feathers   **B.** are   **C.** beautiful

4. My mother bought him.

   A. My   **B.** mother   **C.** bought

Part 2. Proper Nouns

Read the sentence. Choose the noun that needs a capital letter.

5. The chicken laid an egg on sunday.

   A. chicken   **B.** egg   **C.** sunday

6. My sister alice milked the cow.

   A. sister   **B.** alice   **C.** cow

7. We found shells on the beach in august.

   A. shells   **B.** beach   **C.** august

Part 3. Possessive Nouns

Read the sentence. Choose the word that is a possessive noun.

8. Mel's family is having a party.

   A. Mel's   **B.** family   **C.** party

9. That dog has Jane's shoes!

   A. dog   **B.** Jane's   **C.** shoes

Part 4. Common, Proper, or Possessive

Read the sentence. Choose the noun that can be used correctly in the sentence.

10. The _____ dug in the garden

    A. Dogs   **B.** cat's   **C.** rabbits

11. We are going to the beach this _____.

    A. Friday's   **B.** Sunday   **C.** monday

12. _____ voice is beautiful.

    A. Lisa's   **B.** Ellen   **C.** Singers

Unit Checkpoint Learning Coach Instructions
Verbs

Explain that students are going to show what they have learned about identifying and using action verbs.

1. Give students the Unit Checkpoint pages.

2. Read the directions together. If needed, read the questions and answer choices to students. Have students complete the Checkpoint on their own.

3. Use the Answer Key to score the Checkpoint and then enter the results online.

4. Review each exercise with students. Work with students to correct any exercise that they missed.

Unit Checkpoint
Verbs

Part 1. Identify Verbs

Read the sentence. Choose the verb.

1. The car drives down the street.
   A. down   **B.** drives   **C.** car

2. The tractor mows the hay.
   A. tractor   **B.** hay   **C.** mows

3. The boat sails on the water.
   A. sails   **B.** on   **C.** water

Part 2. Use Action Verbs

Read the sentence. Choose the action verb to fill in the blank.

4. Marcus _____ dinner.
   A. food   **B.** oven   **C.** cooks

5. My uncle _____ a story.
   A. word   **B.** tells   **C.** books

6. We _____ at the stars.

    A. look   **B.** sky   **C.** eyes

Part 3. Noun–Verb Agreement

Read the sentences. Choose the sentence where the noun and verb fit together.

7. Which is the correct sentence?

    A. The ducks swim.

    B. The duck swim.

    C. The ducks swims.

8. Which is the correct sentence?

    A. My brother walk on the grass.

    B. My brothers walks on the grass.

    C. My brother walks on the grass.

9. Which is the correct sentence?

    A. The boy throw the ball.

    B. The boy throws the ball.

    C. The boys throws the ball.

Part 4. More Noun–Verb Agreement

Read the sentence. Choose the verb that belongs in the blank.

10. The singers _____ to the music.

    A. listens   **B.** listen

11. The musician _____ the horn.

    A. blows   **B.** blow

12. My friends _____ at the end of the concert.

    A. claps   **B.** clap

Unit Checkpoint Learning Coach Instructions
Pronouns

Explain that students are going to show what they have learned about identifying and using pronouns.

1. Give students the Unit Checkpoint pages.

2. Read the directions together. If needed, read the questions and answer choices to students. Have students complete the Checkpoint on their own.

3. Use the Answer Key to score the Checkpoint and then enter the results online.

4. Review each exercise with students. Work with students to correct any exercise that they missed.

Unit Checkpoint
Pronouns

Part 1. Identify Pronouns
Read the sentence. Choose the pronoun.

1. I am really tired.

   A. am   **B.** I   **C.** really

2. Jane is talking to her dad.

   A. Jane   **B.** to   **C.** her

3. They are in the backyard.

   A. They   **B.** are   **C.** the

4. Everyone was at the game.

   A. Everyone   **B.** was   **C.** at

5. Josh and Dee are putting on their skates.

   A. Dee   **B.** their   **C.** skates

WRITING SKILLS

Part 2. Use Pronouns

Read the sentence. Choose the pronoun to fill in the blank.

6. The snow is falling. _____ looks nice.

   A. They   **B.** It   **C.** Them

7. Todd asks me a question, and _____ answer him.

   A. his   **B.** me   **C.** I

8. The fish are swimming. _____ are fast.

   A. They   **B.** It   **C.** Our

9. Ouch! I stubbed _____ toe!

   A. me   **B.** him   **C.** my

10. The girl cleaned _____ glasses.

   A. you   **B.** her   **C.** them

11. You dropped _____ wallet.

   A. they   **B.** your   **C.** I

WRITING SKILLS

12. The room was quiet. _____ was talking.

   A. Everyone   **B.** Some   **C.** Nobody

13. _____ of the kittens were asleep.

   A. Some   **B.** Everybody   **C.** Anyone

Part 3. Pronoun *I*

Read the sentence. Choose the word that needs a capital letter.

14. May i speak to that girl?

   A. i   **B.** speak   **C.** girl

Unit Checkpoint Learning Coach Instructions
Verb Tense

Explain that students are going to show what they have learned about identifying and using verb tense.

1. Give students the Unit Checkpoint pages.

2. Read the directions together. If needed, read the questions and answer choices to students. Have students complete the Checkpoint on their own.

3. Use the Answer Key to score the Checkpoint and then enter the results online.

4. Review each exercise with students. Work with students to correct any exercise that they missed.

Unit Checkpoint
Verb Tense

Part 1. Identify Verb Tense

Read the sentence. Choose the tense of the underlined verb.

1. We <u>fix</u> our bikes.

   A. past   **B.** present   **C.** future

2. My dad <u>cooked</u> dinner.

   A. past   **B.** present   **C.** future

3. Kim <u>jogs</u> in the park.

   A. past   **B.** present   **C.** future

4. The band <u>will play</u> all night.

   A. past   **B.** present   **C.** future

5. The dog <u>chased</u> the ball.

   A. past   **B.** present   **C.** future

Part 2. Use Past Tense

Read the sentence. Choose the past tense verb to fill in the blank.

6. Last week, my dog _____ at the moon.

    A. howls   **B.** howled   **C.** will howl

7. Yesterday, they _____ an old movie.

    A. show   **B.** will show   **C.** showed

8. Last night, we _____ at the stars.

    A. looks   **B.** looked   **C.** will look

Part 3. Use Present Tense

Read the sentence. Choose the present tense verb to fill in the blank.

9. Right now, he _____ the dog.

    A. will walk   **B.** walked   **C.** walks

10. Today, I _____ with my friends.

    A. play   **B.** played   **C.** will play

WRITING SKILLS

Part 4. Use Future Tense

Read the sentence. Choose the future tense verb to fill in the blank.

11. Next week, I _____ the band.

    A. join   **B.** joined   **C.** will join

12. Tomorrow, Sean _____ his room.

    A. will clean   **B.** cleaned   **C.** cleans

WRITING SKILLS

Unit Checkpoint Learning Coach Instructions
Adjectives

Explain that students are going to show what they have learned about recognizing and using adjectives.

1. Give students the Unit Checkpoint pages.

2. Read the directions together. If needed, read the questions and answer choices to students. Have students complete the Checkpoint on their own.

3. Use the Answer Key to score the Checkpoint and then enter the results online.

4. Review each exercise with students. Work with students to correct any exercise that they missed.

Unit Checkpoint
Adjectives

Part 1. Identify Adjectives
Read the sentence. Choose the adjective.

1. I drank cold water.

   A. drank   **B.** cold   **C.** water

2. That car is going fast.

   A. That   **B.** car   **C.** going

3. I ate all those oranges.

   A. ate   **B.** those   **C.** oranges

4. Our yellow house is over there.

   A. yellow   **B.** over   **C.** there

Part 2. Identify Articles

Read the sentence. Choose the article.

5. Let's go to a movie.

    A. Let's   **B.** go   **C.** a

6. The cat is purring.

    A. The   **B.** cat   **C.** purring

Part 3. Use Adjectives

Read the sentence. Choose an adjective to fill in the blank.

7. I am playing my dad's _____ guitar.

    A. piano   **B.** old   **C.** hat

8. We could see the _____ moon through the window.

    A. cheese   **B.** star   **C.** bright

9. The _____ sky was pretty.

    A. blue   **B.** up   **C.** airplane

WRITING SKILLS

10. Who is _____ person over there?

    A. these   **B.** this   **C.** that

11. May we buy _____ baseball cards?

    A. this   **B.** these   **C.** that

12. Hello, _____ is Gerald speaking.

    A. that   **B.** this   **C.** those

Part 4. Use Articles

Read the sentence. Choose an article to fill in the blank.

13. _____ cookies are ready!

    A. An   **B.** The

14. I think _____ ape just walked by!

    A. a   **B.** an

15. May we take _____ pear from this tree?

    A. a   **B.** an

Unit Checkpoint Learning Coach Instructions
Capital Letters and Punctuation

xplain that students are going to show what they have learned about capital letters
nd punctuation.

1. Give students the Unit Checkpoint pages.

2. Read the directions together. If needed, read the questions and answer choices to
   students. Have students complete the Checkpoint on their own.

3. Use the Answer Key to score the Checkpoint and then enter the results online.

4. Review each exercise with students. Work with students to correct any exercise
   that they missed.

Unit Checkpoint
Capital Letters and Punctuation

Part 1. Identify Contractions
Read the sentence. Choose the word that is a contraction.

1. Bill's dog isn't happy.

   A. Bill's   **B.** isn't   **C.** happy

2. Didn't you go to Kim's house?

   A. Didn't   **B.** you   **C.** Kim's

Part 2. Form and Use Contractions
Read the sentence. Choose the correct contraction to replace the underlined words.

3. We <u>are not</u> eating dessert tonight.

   A. arenot

   B. aren't

4. My brother <u>has not</u> woken up yet.

   A. hasn't

   B. has'nt

5. I <u>could not</u> see the moon last night.

   A. couldn't

   B. could'nt

6. You <u>must not</u> forget to brush your teeth.

   A. musn't

   B. mustn't

Part 3. Separate Words in a Series

Finish the sentence with the answer that uses commas correctly.

7. Wanda loves _____.

   A. cats dogs and hamsters

   B. cats, dogs, and hamsters

   C. cats, dogs and hamsters

8. He collects _____.

   A. rocks shells, and glass

   B. rocks shells and glass

   C. rocks, shells, and glass

9. The flowers were _____.

   A. red, white, blue, and yellow

   B. red white, blue and yellow

   C. red, white, blue and yellow

10. My friends _____.

   A. joke, smile laugh, and talk

   B. joke, smile, laugh, and talk

   C. joke smile laugh and talk

Part 4. Use Capital Letters and Commas

Finish the sentence with the date that uses capital letters and commas correctly. Then, write today's date.

11. My grandfather was born on _____

    A. February 3 1954

    B. February, 3, 1954

    C. February 3, 1954

12. My friends moved on _____

    A. march 22, 2003

    B. March 22 2003

    C. March 22, 2003

13. This painting was made on _____

    A. july 7 1552

    B. July 7, 1552

    C. July 7 1552

14. Today's date is _____

WRITING SKILLS

Semester Checkpoint Learning Coach Instructions
Sentences, Nouns, and Verbs

Explain that students are going to show what they have learned about sentences, nouns, and verbs.

1. Give students the Semester Checkpoint: Sentences, Nouns, and Verbs pages.

2. Read the directions together. If needed, read the questions and answer choices to students. Have students complete the Checkpoint on their own.

3. Use the Answer Key to score the Checkpoint and then enter the results online.

4. Review each exercise with students. Work with students to correct any exercise that they missed.

Semester Checkpoint
Sentences, Nouns, and Verbs

Part 1. Identify the Naming Part
Read the sentence. Choose the naming part.

1. Wolves howled at the moon.

   A. moon   **B.** Wolves   **C.** howled

Part 2. Identify the Action Part
Read the sentence. Choose the action part.

2. Paul and Anya ran outside.

   A. Paul and Anya

   B. Paul

   C. ran outside

Part 3. Identify Complete Sentences
Read the word groups. Choose the complete sentence.

3. Which is the complete sentence?

   A. The full moon in the sky.

   B. The sun is shining.

   C. Looking at the grass in the park.

4. Which is the complete sentence?

   A. All of the dogs outside.

   B. Was playing in the rain.

   C. The beach is closed today.

Part 4. Identify Kinds of Sentences

Read the sentence. Choose what kind of sentence it is.

5. Please clean your room.

   A. statement   C. question

   B. command   D. exclamation

6. I won the game!

   A. statement   C. question

   B. command   D. exclamation

7. What time is the play?

   A. statement   C. question

   B. command   D. exclamation

8. The moon is full tonight.

   A. statement   C. question

   B. command   D. exclamation

Part 5. Choose the End Mark

Choose the end mark that belongs at the end of the sentence.

9. Question: Do you have your boots

   A. . **B.** ? **C.** !

10. Statement: Her hat is on the table

   A. . **B.** ? **C.** !

Part 6. Identify Nouns

Read the sentence. Choose the word that is a noun.

11. The clouds were white and fluffy.

   A. clouds **B.** white **C.** fluffy

12. This August was very hot.

   A. This **B.** August **C.** hot

Part 7. Use Possessive Nouns

Read the sentence. Choose the noun that correctly fills in the blank.

13. We went to my _____ party.

   A. friends **B.** friend's

WRITING SKILLS

Part 8. Use Capital Letters

Read the sentence. Choose the underlined word that needs a capital letter.

14. A <u>bus</u> trip in <u>july</u> will be <u>fun</u>.

    A. bus   **B.** july   **C.** fun

Part 9. Identify Complete Sentences

Choose the sentence that is written correctly.

5. Which sentence is written correctly?

    A. We looked at Ella's painting

    B. We looked at Ella's painting.

    C. we looked at Ella's painting

16. Which sentence is written correctly?

    A. We wrote a letter to Zach in April.

    B. we wrote a letter to Zach in April

    C. We wrote a letter to Zach in April

WRITING SKILLS

Part 10. Identify Verbs

Read the sentence. Choose the word that is a verb.

17. The truck blows its horn.

    A. truck   **B.** blows   **C.** horn

18. The cats and dogs fight all night.

    A. cats   **B.** dogs   **C.** fight

Part 11. Identify Noun–Verb Agreement

Read the sentence. Choose the sentence where the noun and verb fit together.

19. Which sentence is written correctly?

    A. Boris laugh.

    B. Boris laughs.

20. Which sentence is written correctly?

    A. Birds chirp.

    B. Birds chirps.

Semester Checkpoint Learning Coach Instructions

Pronouns, Verb Tense, Adjectives, Capital Letters, and Punctuation

Explain that students are going to show what they have learned about pronouns, verb tense, adjectives, capital letters, and punctuation.

1. Give students the Semester Checkpoint: Pronouns, Verb Tense, Adjectives, Capital Letters, and Punctuation pages.

2. Read the directions together. If needed, read the questions and answer choices to students. Have students complete the Checkpoint on their own.

3. Use the Answer Key to score the Checkpoint and then enter the results online.

4. Review each exercise with students. Work with students to correct any exercise that they missed.

Semester Checkpoint
Pronouns, Verb Tense, Adjectives, Capital Letters, and Punctuation

WRITING SKILLS

Part 1. Identify the Pronoun
Read the sentence. Choose the pronoun in the sentence.

1. Grandpa put on his tie.

   A. Grandpa   **B.** his   **C.** tie

2. They shared a piece of pie.

   A. They   **B.** piece   **C.** of

Part 2. Replace Nouns with Pronouns
Read the sentence. Choose the correct pronoun to replace the underlined word or words.

3. I was talking to <u>Mike</u>.

   A. them   **B.** you   **C.** him

4. That is <u>Wendy's</u> hat.

   A. her   **B.** she   **C.** our

5. <u>Lisa and I</u> played tag.

   A. She   **B.** We   **C.** They

Part 3. Present Tense

Choose the present tense verb to fill in the blank.

6. Right now, we _____ outside.

    A. hiked   **B.** will hike   **C.** hike

Part 4. Past Tense

Choose the past tense verb to fill in the blank.

7. Yesterday, you _____ baseball.

    A. played   **B.** play   **C.** will play

Part 5. Future Tense

Choose the future tense verb to fill in the blank.

8. Tonight, I _____ a picture.

    A. will paint   **B.** painted   **C.** paint

WRITING SKILLS

WRITING SKILLS

Part 6. Verb Tense
Choose the tense of the underlined verb.

9. I <u>will hop</u> like a bunny.
   - **A.** past tense
   - **B.** present tense
   - **C.** future tense

10. She <u>climbs</u> the tree.
   - **A.** past tense
   - **B.** present tense
   - **C.** future tense

Part 7. Identify Adjectives
Read the sentence. Choose the adjective in the sentence.

11. Bright lights hurt my eyes.
   - **A.** Bright
   - **B.** hurt
   - **C.** eyes

12. I love that movie!
   - **A.** I
   - **B.** love
   - **C.** that

Part 8. Capital Letters
Read the sentence. Choose the word that needs a capital letter.

13. Mother said i can go to the game.
   - **A.** i
   - **B.** go
   - **C.** game

Part 9. Articles

Choose the correct article to complete the sentence.

14. The zoo has _____ elephant.

    A. a   **B.** an

15. I am wearing _____ coat.

    A. a   **B.** an

Part 10. Identify Contractions

Read the sentence. Choose the word that is a contraction.

16. We didn't bring a ball!

    A. We   **B.** didn't   **C.** a

Part 11. Use Contractions

Choose the correct contraction to replace the underlined words.

17. Mark <u>is not</u> happy.

    A. isn't   **B.** isnt

18. The sun <u>has not</u> set yet.

    A. hasnot   **B.** hasn't

Part 12. Words in a Series

Choose the words that use commas correctly to complete the sentence.

19. My sister was wearing _____.

    A. socks shoes, gloves, and glasses

    B. socks, shoes, gloves and glasses

    C. socks, shoes, gloves, and glasses

Part 13. Dates

Choose the correctly written date.

20. Choose the correctly written date.

    A. May 4 1977

    B. may 4, 1977

    C. May 4, 1977